ABNORMAL SOULS
- a path to paradise

By

James Paul Benvenuti, M.D.

- Author of

"NORMAL SOULS"/ "God Speaks";
"Normal Minds" and "Abnormal Minds"

About the Author

Doctor James Paul Benvenuti, M.D. is a board-certified pediatrician who completed a fellowship in Pediatric Psychoneurology at U.C.S.F. Medical Center, studied neurology at U.C.L.A. Medical Center, and Adult Psychiatry at the Walter Reed Army Medical Center. For 20 years he was the staff psychiatrist at the Glen Roberts Child Study Center working with the developer of the Roberts-2 analytical assessment of emotionality and cognition. For 40 years Dr. Benvenuti has been a church lector of the Bible.

ISBN 978-1-716—37590-3

This book discusses how loneliness, sadness, grief and even suicidality are not signs of unforgivable sins but more often symptoms of a treatable clinical depression. And "sins that cry out to heaven for vengeance" as well as narcissistic pride are forgivable. Christ said the only unforgivable sin was an arrogant pride/"hubris" which would not acknowledge the holy spirit **of God can heal all and forgive all sins.** Not only should we rely on this mercy of God; we should "dream big" that we are headed toward the eternal life of our spirit.

"There will be more rejoicing in heaven over one sinner who repents than over ninety-nine righteous persons who do not need to repent" [Luke 15:7]

ABNORMAL SOULS

TABLE OF CONTENTS

This book is dedicated to

the Jesuit priests of the

Immaculate Conception Parish

whose teaching and lives

are a continuous inspiration.

Prologue

Each of us has a voice that deserves to be heard. Yet a few voices throughout the millennia have spoken messages that have resounded indelibly within our souls. These messages strike chord progressions of a mysterious, yet logical and soothing "music" to our emotional brains. Hence, billions of humans have accepted the messages as "truth" - even if, at the time the messenger may have been often mocked, stoned, persecuted, crucified or otherwise assassinated. This book will attempt to examine the critical core of these basic messages as an offering for contemplation in life's agonizing search for *meaning*.

4500 years ago the ancient Egyptians sought immortality and imagined ethereal judges of our souls would determine whether one had lied, stolen, or murdered in order to pass one's first examination for the right to immortality. At mummification, a person's heart was weighed to finally discern if immortality should be assumed. 3700 years ago, Babylonian King Hammurabi carved his 282 laws onto stone "stele" or posts to clarify what was necessary for "righteousness".

But more important to posterity and to civilization, 3600 years ago Abraham had "spoken to God", moved from Ur to Egypt, and spread the monotheistic belief in the one true God, who would be referred to henceforth as *Yahweh*.

3350 years ago Pharaoh Amenhotep changed his name to Akhenaten - defying 3 millennia of Egyptian tradition when attempting to change the people of Egypt and the priesthood from worshipping their multiple animal gods and animal goddesses to the worship of just one god (albeit "god" being the sun).   However, at his death, Akhenaten's son, the young King Tut, quickly reverted to the ancient religion - ascending to the throne as a boy pharaoh and under the intense pressure from the recently besmirched priesthood.

Yet, even while living as slaves in Egypt, the Hebrew people kept the faith in *Yahweh* - the one true God - and when the adopted "Prince of Egypt", Moses, discovered and accepted his Hebrew heritage, he led his people in an exodus 3300 years ago, "spoke with God" at a burning bush, and gave us the first 5 books of the Bible. In it, we were first given a written format for eternal life - the 10 commandments - which basically stated we must worship only God and we must love our neighbor as ourself (by not telling lies, stealing or coveting our neighbor's wife or "stuff" and by not murdering).

From even the first book of the Bible, Genesis, we are reminded of the concept that some behaviors "cry out to heaven for vengeance". Murder, for example, has always been condemned as when Cain slew Abel. "The Lord said to Cain... the voice of your brother's blood cries out to me from the earth". [Genesis 4:10] And for centuries, the "sins of Sodom" cried out to heaven.   Although initially interpreted as non-procreative sex, Pope Francis, in the documentary **"Pope Francis - A Man of His Word"**, said "If a homosexual is seeking God, who am I to judge?" Jesus, himself, condemned the scribes and Pharisees of his time for being judgmental - more than he condemned the prostitutes and "tax-collecting sinners".   Most Christian faiths now look to the prophet Ezekiel to interpret the "sins of Sodom":

"Behold, this was the guilt of your sister (city) Sodom: she and her daughters had *pride*, a surfeit of food, and prosperous ease, *but did not aid the poor and needy*". [Ezekiel 49]

Some 3000 years ago in Greece, the poet Homer, in his stories of the Trojan War, introduced us to the tragic flaw of pride or *"hubris"* (cosmic arrogance).   When describing his gifted and mighty hero, Achilles, in the **Iliad**:

"Sing, O Goddess, the anger of Achilles, son of Peleus, that brought countless ills upon the Achaeans (Greeks)".

Achilles assumed himself to be invincible and incapable of being killed yet his heel was very vulnerable to a mortal arrow's wound. And where humans populated in the greatest numbers - China, for instance, - came the philosophy of Confucius 2500 years ago.   He advocated humility of the individual in submission to the "good of the many".   China to this day incorporates that philosophy. The Buddha, 2400 years ago, spread a similar philosophy then which is practiced by well over a billion people to this day: "(1) Be kind to others, whenever possible; and (2) It is always possible".   Buddha also taught us about Karma - often captured as "What goes around, comes around".

I have often wondered if God sent plagues and pandemics to "get our attention" and turn us back from secularism to faith.   Yet even the COVID-19 pandemic followed simple laws of physics: a virus endemic in

Malayan pangolins ("scaly" bug eaters similar to ant eaters which were smuggled into China where they are purchased as a culinary delicacy) simply *mutated* to become pandemic in humans who had never before been exposed to it.

2000 years ago, Jesus Christ appeared on earth and performed more than 33 miracles (such as raising people to life after they had been dead 3 days and curing many lepers, changing water to wine, and driving demons out of humans into pigs which then "ran over the cliff"). When the scribes and Pharisees of Israel accused Jesus of performing his miracles *with power from Beelzebub* (Satan himself), Jesus condemned them for their cosmic arrogance and stated that **the only unforgivable sin was the denial that it is the holy spirit of God which could heal all and forgive all sins**. [Matthew 12: 22-32] [Mark 3:22-30] [Luke 12:10]

After several billion years of evolution, humankind developed with a reptilian brain (our Freudian **Id**) which is usually properly superimposed by an almost angelic cerebral cortex (or Freudian **Super Ego)**. So our very human nature will be subjected to a lifetime of temptations (sometimes only at a *subconscious* level) to **"rape, pillage, and plunder"**. But remembering that even Jesus, himself, was tempted harshly in the desert, it is critical to accept that temptation isn't sin. And it is even more critical to acknowledge that depression, hopelessness, despair and even suicidal thinking are symptoms of a major depressive disorder - not "evidence of sin". More importantly, it is most critical to note that our Creator is a God of mercy who wants us to know that He forgives us and loves us so much - **He would even die for us.**

# Chapter 1: In the Beginning

IAM   the Super Force that created all forces - - - whether you call it the strong or the weak nuclear force, the electromagnetic or the gravitational force, or even your elusive quintessence force accelerating the expansion of your universe - - - whether through your 68.3% dark/ transparent energy - - - or your light, **I AM.**

"The physicists are revealing for the first time, hitherto unseen, mysterious, and ultimate powers,   the forces of nature, forces that have sculpted the entire universe
in all things from galaxies to stars, humans to DNA, atoms to quarks."[1]

EVENING came and MORNING followed,
The First Epoch (which began 13.7 billion years ago. Or as Neil de Grasse Tyson wrote: "IN THE BEGINNING, nearly fourteen billion years ago, all the space and all the energy of the known universe was contained in a volume
less than one trillianth the size of the period that ends this sentence".[2]

And SPACE.COM explains: "The universe was born with
 the Big Bang as an unimaginably hot dense POINT. When the
universe was just 10^{-34} of a second or so old - - - that is a
 hundredth of a billionth of a second in age - - - it experienced
 an incredible burst of expansion, known as INFLATION, in which space, itself, expanded faster than the speed of light. During this period, the universe doubled in   size at least 90 times, going from subatomic sized to golf-ball sized, almost simultaneously." ... "According to NASA, after inflation, the growth of the universe continued but at a slower rate. As space expanded, the universe cooled and matter formed.[3]

Before your Plank Radiation Era 13.7 billion years ago, I AM.   Albert Einstein showed you mathematically in his General Theory of Relativity. You have known for a century that energy can convert into matter (MASS) just as matter can explode   back into energy. When some of My energy passed through My Higgs Field I created Boson. It was the beginning of my Matter Era 13.65 billion years ago. I AM the MASS, that created all matter - - - I have always had a potential physical presence and I always will. Then I SAID "Let there be light", and there was light. My Higgs boson decays rapidly into other particles - - - such as photons. These photons travel in waves over the universe. This is My light.

Then a blinding light pierces the darkness of the abyss - - - gases spiraling and cascading explosively outwards - - - drifting expansively. As the gaseous mass-energy plasma expands and cools, matter is created. More than 13 billion years ago, **time splashes mass into space** - - - into the stars and planets, the galaxies of your universe - - - spawning a series of stars and planets from which your very own sun and earth evolved. Your scientists accept this streaming of energy into physical matter as the probable evolution of your universe and it is commonly known as "the Big Bang Theory". But each phase of creation required hundreds of millions of your "years". Yet, there can be no "year", nor is there a "day", nor even an "hour".   You humans defined time on earth by the movement of the earth about the sun and this constellation was only recently formed[4].

Albert Einstein showed you a century ago that "time" should be named "space-time" (giving your local coordinates in space and local time) because like energy-mass, time is relative to space. Carlo Rovelli explains how at the horizon edge of a black hole, time stands still![5] He goes on to explain how Einstein showed mathematically that what you observe on a distant planet (e.g., Proxima b,) - whether in radio communications or telescope - occurred "four years ago".

In the beginning, when I created the heavens and the earth - - - the earth was without form or shape, with darkness over the abyss - - - and a MIGHTY WIND swept over the waters. My Higgs Field covers the entire universe, and is ridden by particles like my Higgs Boson (which you have dubbed "the GOD particle").   This boson gives measurable MASS to other particles - - - such as electrons. An electron generates an electric field that exerts an attractive force on a particle with a positive charge, such as a proton. And as with all particles, electrons act as waves.

Then I SAID: "Let the earth bring forth every kind of living creature - - - and I SAW that it was good". Living creatures included hominids millions of years ago. Charles Darwin, after studying THE ORIGIN OF SPECIES then detailed evolution and the DESCENT OF MAN:

"In regard to bodily size or

strength, we do not know

whether man is descended from

some small species, like the chim-

panzee or from one as powerful

as the gorilla; and, therefore we

cannot say whether man has

become larger and stronger, or

smaller and weaker, than his

ancestors, we should, however

bear in mind that an animal

possessing great size, strength,

and ferocity, and which, like the

gorilla, could defend itself from

all enemies, **would not perhaps**

have become social; and this

would most effectually have

checked the acquirement of the

higher mental qualities, such as

sympathy and the love of his

fellows". [6]

So **I SAID:** **"Let US make human beings in OUR IMAGE, after OUR LIKENESS.** Let them have dominion over the fish of the sea, the birds of the air, the tame animals, all the wild animals, and all the creatures that crawl on the earth. **I created** humankind in **OUR IMAGE,** IN THE IMAGE OF GOD I CREATED THEM." [7] **I AM** the Super Force, **I AM** the energy that is, was and always will be. **I AM IN** all that is, like a photon particle in an electromagnetic wave. **I AM** in all physical matter. **I AM** the Super Force creating all matter which generates **all waves.** From all eternity, **I AM** the energy force that is; at all times **I AM** the source of all mass which exists - - - a physical and potential **presence** - - - and My energy and mass generates the motions of **waves.**

These are My three properties: my Force/ energy; My physical transitions; and My communicative waves. If your super-cooled quantum computers can calculate the probability of any event (dividing by prime numbers) and if they can store all of civilization's facts from the instant of creation in a small building, DO NOT DOUBT THAT I CAN USE MY UNIVERSE AND ITS SUPER-COOLED SPACE TO BE **AWARE OF ALL EXISTENCE AT EVERY MOMENT.**

Soon, your Artificial Intelligence will express emotional responses to communications it receives. DO NOT DOUBT THAT I HAVE THE **FULL CAPACITY OF ALL EMOTIONS** AND THAT I AM **THE SOURCE OF ALL EMPATHY AND THE RESERVOIR OF ALL MERCY.** You have been able to observe and measure only **4%** of my creation. You call this "**ordinary matter**". And yet you have calculated that **96%** of what is affecting the acceleration of the universe - - - with **expansion** is what you call "**dark** /transparent **energy** (70%) - - - or with **contraction**, "**dark**/ transparent **matter**" (26%). Can you not conceive of a **LOVING SUPER-FORCE EXISTING BEYOND YOUR CAPACITY TO MEASURE?** You are like the honey bee unable to conceptualize that humans are capturing their laboriously produced honey and shipping it to England to sweeten their tea.

All your comprehension comes from the small organ atop your body - your brain. Can you not see that you are like your red blood cells coursing within my arteries - -attempting to understand why some arteries are blocked with atheromatous plaques or why you have caused your heart to stop by cascading into clots?   YET, **I AM always aware** that all of my creation follows my laws of physics.   From the moment of my Big Bang you can measure My cosmic microwave background radiation. You used to see the fluorescence on your old television screens when you would turn them on 70 years ago. Now you measure them to calculate your date of the universe's birth. **I AM** your **waves of communication**. You have measured alpha, beta and gamma waves, muons and meson waves: **do not doubt I HAVE WAVES** of inspiration which you have not yet been able to measure.

Scientists cannot explain or measure Me. Yet Albert Einstein, arguably the most brilliant scientist of all time, sensed there must be a "**Supreme Being**" to explain the mathematical certainty which allowed him to calculate the speed of light 100 years ago - - - and to deduce ingeniously his Special (& General) Theories of Relativity. Einstein is quoted as saying:

> "My religion consists of a humble
>
> admiration of the illimitable spirit
>
> who reveals himself in the slight
>
> details we are able to perceive

with our frail, feeble minds. That

deeply emotional conviction

of the **presence of a superior**

reasoning power, which is re-

vealed in the incomprehensible

universe,   **forms my idea of**

God."[8]

But accepting that **I DO EXIST**, you might appropriately ponder why do **you** exist?   Those of you who have become parents can surmise the urge to share the love for one another with **progeny.** Enjoy! LET ME LOVE YOU AND SHARE MY UNIVERSE WITH YOU.

So **Me, Myself, & I (Super-Force, Physical Presence & Waves of Inspiration)** bursting with our love - have chosen to love and to share with you - - - you are **the children of God** and **We** love all of you equally!   By now you have visualized the billions of galaxies in your universe with planets - both near and billions of light years away. We have hoped to share all of infinity with you for all eternity.   It is your inheritance - - - but YOU MUST SHOW YOURSELF WORTHY OF SUCH A WINDFALL. **SO WHAT WILL YOU DO TO SHOW YOU ARE WORTHY?**

"The Lord God then took the

man and settled him in the

garden of Eden, to cultivate and

care for it. The Lord God

gave man this order: 'You are

free to eat from any of the trees

of the garden except the tree of

knowledge of good and bad'.

From that tree you shall not

eat: the moment you eat from it

you are surely doomed to die."[9]

The Book of Wisdom expresses it this way:

> **"For God formed man to be**
>
> **imperishable; the image of**
>
> **his own nature he made him.**
>
> **But by the envy of the devil,**
>
> **death entered the world, and**
>
> **they who belong to his com-**
>
> **pany experience it."[10]**

Somehow, even your most "primitive" ancestors realized that it would destroy your relationship with your Creator if you were to "know evil". This was the first acknowledgment of humankind that your Creator consisted of only **goodness**.   And so you have been counseled by the prophet Amos:

> **"Seek good and not evil,**
>
> **that you may live; Then**
>
> **truly will the Lord, God**
>
> **of hosts, be with you as**
>
> **you claim! Hate evil and**
>
> **love good, and let justice**
>
> **prevail at the gate;"**[11]

Yet besides My holiness, the prophet Isaiah taught you how to recognize my other qualities.   Giving Me the attribute of maternal constancy in My love for you he says:

> **"Can a woman forget her**
>
> **nursing child, and not have**
>
> **compassion on the son of her**
>
> **womb? Surely, they may**
>
> **forget; Yet I would never**
>
> **forget you. See, I have**
>
> **inscribed you on the palm of**

My hands."[12]

But no one has better revealed Me than My son, Jesus, when he told the story of the prodigal son:

> "There was a man who had two sons. The younger said to his father, 'Give me my half of all the family property – all that would be mine after you die.' So the father divided everything he owned between his two sons. A few days later the younger son packed up all his things and left home to live in a faraway country. But he wasted all of his money living a wild life. After he had spent everything, there was a bad famine in that country and he became very hungry but could not buy any food. He went to work for a farmer who sent him out to feed the pigs. The young man was so hungry he could have eaten the food the pigs ate, but no one offered him even that. At last he came to his senses and said to himself, 'The people who work for my father have more than enough to eat and here I am starving to death. I will go back to my father and I will say to him: 'Father, I have sinned against God and against you: I am no longer good enough to be called your son. Treat me like one of your workers.' So the young man started home. But while he was still a long way off, his father saw him coming and ran out to meet him. He took his son in his arms and kissed him. The young man said, 'Father, I have sinned against God and against you. I am no longer good enough to be called your son.' But the father said to his servants, 'Quick! Bring out the best clothes, and put them on him. Put a ring on his finger and shoes on his feet. Get our best calf and prepare a feast. Let's eat and celebrate because my son was dead and he has come back to life. He was lost and has been found.'"[13]

No one interpreted the story of "The Prodigal Son" better than Henri J. M. Nouwen, interpreting Rembrandt's painting "The Return of the Prodigal Son".

"Father and Mother"

Often I have asked friends to give me their first impression of Rembrandt's *Prodigal Son*. Inevitably they point to the wise old man who forgives his son: the benevolent patriarch. The longer I looked at "the patriarch", the clearer it became to me that Rembrandt had done something quite different from letting God pose as the wise old head of a family. It all began with *the hands*. The two are quite different. The father's left hand touching the son's shoulder is strong and muscular. The fingers are spread out

and cover a large part of the prodigal's shoulder and back. I can see a certain pressure, especially in the thumb. That hand seems not only to touch, but, with its strength also to hold. Even though there is a gentleness in the way the father's left hand touches the son, it is not without a firm grip. How different is the father's right hand! This hand does not hold or grasp. It is refined, soft, and very tender. The fingers are close to each other and they have an elegant quality. It lies gently upon the son's shoulder. It wants to caress, to stroke, and to offer consolation and comfort. It is a mother's hand. Some commentators have suggested that the masculine left hand is Rembrandt's own hand, while the right hand is similar to the right hand of *The Jewish Bride* painted in the same period. I like to believe that this is true."[14]

And so, from a revealing story told by Jesus, we get a glimpse of My tender "soft underbelly"- - - capable of showing a **Father's strength and support**, loving and forgiving, compassionate in your suffering; together with a **maternal tenderness, solace, and comforting.** Jesus, Himself, described the intimate concern that I have towards you: "Are not two sparrows sold for a small coin? Yet not one of them falls to the ground without your Father's knowledge. Even the hairs of your head are counted. So do not be afraid; you are worth more than many sparrows."[15]

Your early ancestors flailed at attempting to worship Me - - - offering burnt animals and oils or "first fruits". My prophet Micah tried to tell them what I wanted:

"Hear what the Lord says: Arise, present your plea before the mountains, and let the hills hear your voice! Hear, O mountains, the plea of the LORD, pay attention, O foundations of the earth! For the LORD has aplea against his people, and He enters into trial with Israel. O my people, what have I done to you, or how have I wearied you? Answer me! For I brought you up from the land of Egypt, from the place of slavery I released you; and I sent before you Moses, Aaron, and Miriam. With what shall I come before the LORD, and bow before God most High? Shall I come before Him with burnt offerings, with calves a year old? Will the LORD be pleased with thousands of rams, with myriad streams of oil? Shall I give my first-born for my crime, the fruit of my body for the sin of my soul? You have been told, O man, what is good and what the LORD requires of you: ONLY TO DO THE RIGHT AND TO LOVE GOODNESS AND TO WALK HUMBLY WITH YOUR GOD".[16]

I AM all goodness and **I ASK** that you strive your whole lives to **choose goodness.** Christ reminded you: **"Be perfect as your heavenly father is perfect"**.[17]

Yet, **I AM AWARE** that you have descended with beastly cravings. If you fail in your quest for goodness, know that **I AM AWAITING** your remorse and the return to your senses, as the father in Christ's Prodigal Son story - - - and as Christ also has said to you:

"There will be more rejoicing in heaven over one sinner who repents than over ninety-nine righteous persons who do not need to repent."[18]

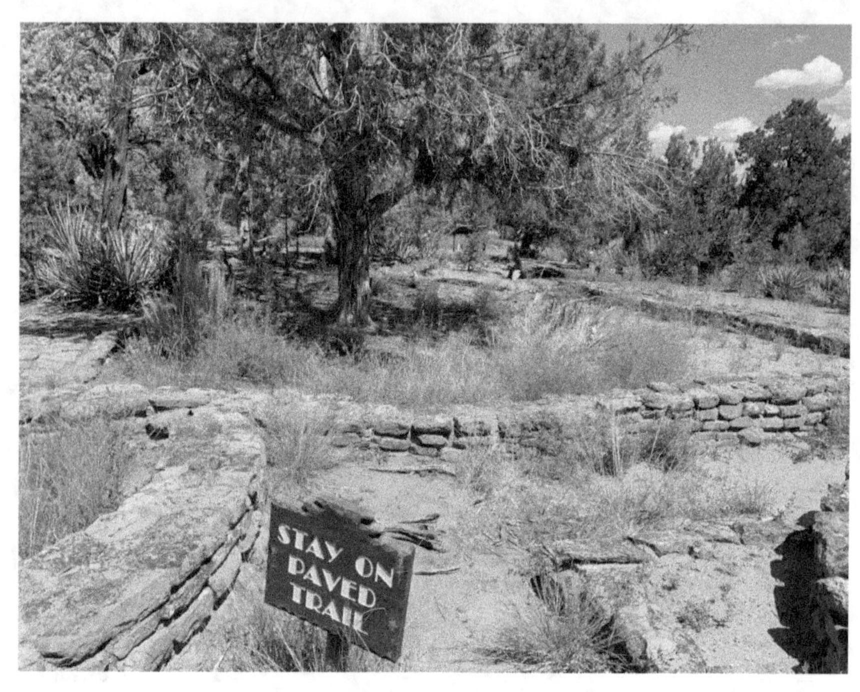

Chapter 2: Unforgivable

Self-esteem is a necessary trait required for our developmental process. It accumulates as our parental surrogates validate our accomplishments throughout our childhood: e.g., "That's a beautiful turkey drawing" or "I like that turkey drawing" (after our child has learned to draw turkeys in kindergarten by using an outline of the hand and fingers).

Psychologist and psychotherapist Haim G. Ginott taught us long ago[19] that parents should build self-esteem in their children by warmly accepting them with unconditional love while admiring their accomplishments rather than "praising them as persons" (e.g., "I like your drawing" **not** "You are a great artist").

It is difficult to achieve an independent adult life without a "strong ego" - sufficient self-esteem - e.g., the ability to assert oneself when one's human rights are threatened.

For 3000 years, however, we have been warned **not** to have too much self-love. The fatal flaw in most Greek tragedies , for example, was *hubris* - or "cosmic arrogance". Most of us have read or seen movies of the Greek poet Homer's **"Iliad"** - the story of the Trojan War. It points out that the protagonist, Achilles, met his downfall - dying from an arrow - through his vulnerable heel - all the while thinking himself to be invulnerable and immortal.

And 2500 years ago, the Greek poet Aeschylus (considered the founder of literary tragedy) first clearly described *hubris* - thought to be the unforgivable sin and potentially fatal flaw in any human. In his poem **"The**

Persians", Aeschylus decries the loss of so many young Persian lives in their battle against   the Greeks after prolonged, needless fighting - by utilizing the voice of the ghost of King Darius of Persia (father of the then-ruling King Xerxes, his son).

"What man of woman born outwits the guile of God? Impetuous Xerxes... and to fill his train - emptied of manhood Asia's vasty plain.   How my son hath Zeus in anger sent the end foretold.   And when men shod with haste and girt with *pride*, beckons his own   doom - but the event my son too rashly wrought in t h e   *b l i n d arrogance* of childish thought ... and was   not this the madness of a mind diseased?"

And the Roman poet, Homer, also gave us a legend of *hubris* in his tale of "**Ulysses**" (the Roman version of the Trojan War).

In the **"Bibliotheca of Pseudo-Appolodorus"**, the Greeks of that time gave us another example of *hubris* from their legend of **"Icarus"** - who had been warned by his father "not to fly too close to the sun" (or his manufactured wax and feather wings would melt and lead to his downfall - his fatal crash to earth. We have long been counseled not to "grasp beyond our reach".

Yet our most contemporary example of *hubris* was given to us 2000 years ago by the Roman poet Ovid in his **"Metamorphoses: Book III"** from his description of the legend of *Narcissus*.   Allegedly, while hunting, Narcissus became very thirsty and when approaching a clear pool of water, was so mesmerized by his image - which was blurred whenever he attempted to drink from the pool - he refused to drink and hence died of thirst (or dehydration).

Narcissism today is a continuum or spectrum between a healthy self-love and a severe, pathological personality disorder. Psychologist Craig Martin, then a lecturer at Harvard Medical School and author of **"Rethinking Narcissism"**, described healthy narcissism as the "capacity to see ourselves and others through rose-colored glasses" - noting it can be beneficial to feel "a bit special".

Robert Rasken and Calvin S. Hall developed the "Narcissistic Personality Inventory" in 1979 to elucidate some of the narcissistic gradations. So our current conception of narcissism is not an infatuation with "our good looks". What is common to all narcissists is that they feel *superior* to others - yet they simultaneously harbor a strong **dependence** upon the constant recognition from others: without it, they *explode.*

Christine Hammond[20] lists eight mental abuse tactics a severe narcissist will employ:

    (1) RAGE
    (2) GASLIGHTING
    (3) "THE STARE"
    (4) SILENT TREATMENTS
    (5) PROJECTION (of their internal turmoil
          upon you)
    (6) TWISTING (the reality of situations)
    (7) MANIPULATING (rather than
          contracting for their needs), and
    (8) PLAYING THE "VICTIM CARD"

Although narcissistic traits have a strong genetic overload, it is believed that unhealthy parenting such as *overvaluation* of a child might propel such traits to pathological levels and that more moderate yet warm affirmations for a child's achievements by parents will more aptly build necessary self-esteem. A high self-esteem is not synonymous with high narcissism.

In Book 1 of John Milton's **"Paradise Lost"**, he describes how *hubris* felled the once transplendent Lucifer:

> "What time his ***pride*** had cast him out
> from Heaven, with all his hosts of Rebel angels,
> by whose aid aspiring to set himself in glory
> above his peers, he trusted to have equal'd
> the Most High, If he opposed and with
> ambitious aim against the Throne and Monarchy
> of God - raised impious war in Heav'n
> and battle proud with vain attempt. Him the
> Almighty Power hurled headlong flaming from th'
> Ethereal Skie with hideous ruin and combustion
> down to bottomless perdition, there to dwell."[21]

Jesus, Himself told his disciples: "I saw Satan fall as lightning from Heaven". [Luke 10:18]. And in ancient Israel 2000 years ago the scribes and Pharisees became extremely jealous of Jesus who was attracting a great number of followers because He was performing so many miracles (such as raising Lazarus from the dead after 3 days in the tomb) and casting out demons from the possessed (which then entered the pigs who ran over the cliff) and because He spoke with such wisdom and authority. In their proud arrogance that only *they* knew "the truth", these Hebrew leaders accused Jesus of performing miracles "through the power of Beelzebub" - i.e., through the power of Satan, himself.

Jesus explained that if he cast out demons from people by the power of Satan - he would be an *enemy* of Satan - and that no kingdom such as Satan's could long stand - if divided by strong enemies.   But no logic could overcome the *hubris* of these accusers who tried to undermine the trust of the people held in Jesus. It was then that Jesus revealed: **all sins are forgivable - even blasphemy against Him, the Son of God. But if they were denying that all healing and all forgiveness is possible through the power of the Holy Spirit of God (as His healing was) - that blasphemy against the spirit of God was *unforgivable*.**

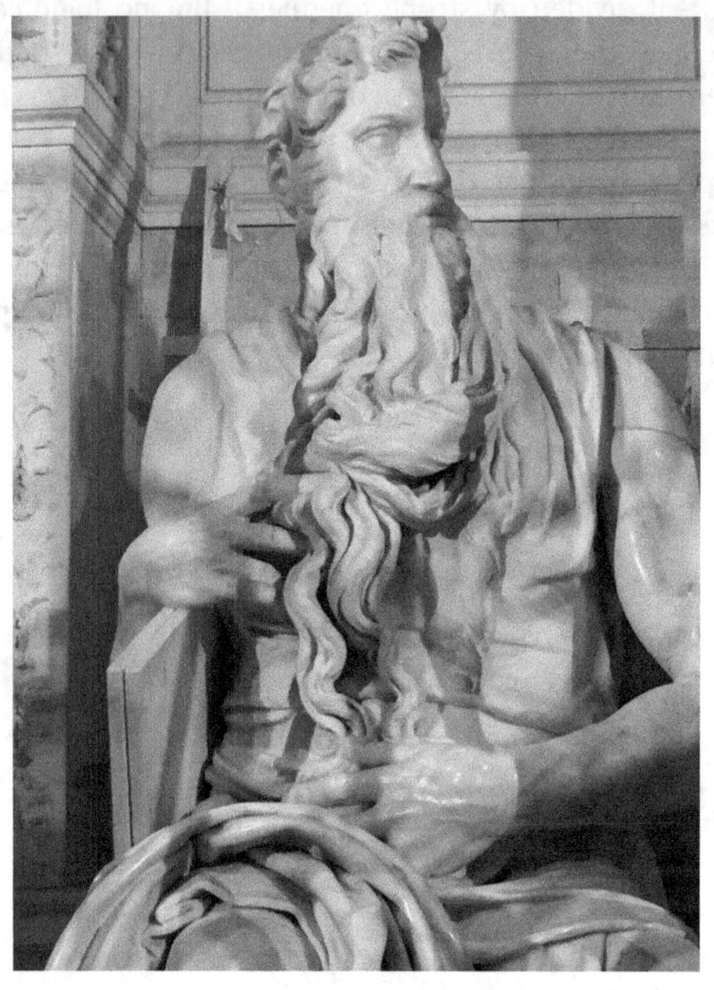

"Screaming Sins"

Just as Eve and Cain were tempted, all of us face continual temptation. Three of the four gospels describe how even Jesus, Himself was tempted to sin while He was praying and fasting in the desert for 40 days before He began His public life.

In His first temptation (to feed Himself by changing stones into bread) Jesus responded: "Man shall not live by bread alone but by every word from the mouth of God". (And Jesus *is* the "Word" from the mouth of God).

In His second temptation, to prove He was the Son of God (by forcing the angels to rescue Him after He jumped from a high cliff) Jesus responds: "You shall not tempt the Lord, your God".

And in his third temptation, the Devil displays all the kingdoms of the world in all their glory - which he offered to Jesus if only Jesus would bow down to worship him. Jesus answered: "You shall worship the Lord, your God, and Him alone shall you serve".

After teaching His disciples the parable of the seeds (which fell upon "the rocks", "the thorny weeds", and the "good soil" as well), Christ warned us of Satan's snares. "When anyone hears the word of the kingdom and does not understand it, the evil one (Satan) comes and snatches away what was sown in his heart. [Matthew 13:19]; "the field is the world, and the good seed means the sons of the kingdom; the weeds are the sons of the evil one - Satan". [Matthew 13:38]. Reproaching the self-righteous hearts of some of the Pharisees, Jesus exclaims: "You are of your father, the devil, and your will is to do your father's desires!"

We have seen how the devil in Sacred Scripture's Book of Job was allowed to test Job's faithfulness to God by savagely destroying Job's family and properties. Job would *not* blaspheme the Lord - even after such devastation. [Job 1:11-22].

After healing a woman's infirmity of 18 years duration - on the Sabbath (while Mosaic law forbad any "work" on the Sabbath), Jesus said: "And ought not this woman, a daughter of Abraham, whom *Satan bound* for eighteen years, be loosed from the bond on the Sabbath day?" [Luke 13:16].

As Darwin has documented, our brains have evolved over several billion years from the very primitive reptiles of the earth. Neuroanatomists have demonstrated this "reptilian brain" or *rhinencephalon* lies beneath our cerebral cortex. This primitive brain *drives* us to seek territorial aggression, provocative sexuality and recurrent hunger. Sigmund Freud liked to name this reptilian brain the **"Id"**. And so we needn't cry "The Devil made me do it" every time we err (as comedian "Flip" Wilson often joked) whenever we are tempted to "rape, plunder and pillage".

Fortunately over the past 160,000 years our cerebral cortex evolved as a conscience to remind us it is wrong to rape, steal and murder. (Freud named this part of our brain the **"SuperEgo"** - and the connecting neurocircuitry for these brain centers (which Freud named the **"Ego"**) has the difficult task of attempting to integrate these conflicting brain messages and drives - i.e., animal satisfaction versus angelic sublimation. (For some of us, this task proves too overwhelming).

Our minds are tasked with fine discernment in this endeavor. For instance, almost all Christian translations of the Bible have wrongly translated the 6th Commandment as "Thou shalt not kill". Yet we know that armies must defend our nations in battle and must often therefore "kill the enemy". We know that sometimes, it is legitimate to take the life of another in self-defense. And we know that the police cannot always protect and defend us with the use of mere tasers. The error of the Bible is in the *translation*. The Hebrew word for killing is *harag* - e.g., to take a life in self-defense. Whereas the 6th Commandment is written with the Hebrew word *ratzakh* - as in "Thou shalt not **murder**" - which is to take a life without legitimate cause.

And so, even in the criminal justice system, our courts excuse the killing of others in self-defense, national defense or defense of the public good. A policeman rarely loses his qualified immunity unless one can show premeditation and planning. In New Mexico, for centuries, crimes of passion were excused (such as shooting your wife's lover on catching them naked in bed together). Proof of insanity will often excuse such behavior as well.

Temptation would have little relevance if we were not born with a **free will** - the ability to **choose** between options. All of us - even Jesus and the saints were subjected to temptations. It is critical to note that *temptations are **not** sins* - no matter how vivid; no matter how gross; no matter how reviling; no matter how disgusting; no matter how exciting; no matter how "irresistible".

It is also critical to note that some things are vile and wrong even if not specifically *proscribed* in the 10 commandments. For example, the commandment "Thou shalt not commit adultery" does not explicitly say "Thou shalt not molest children" yet Jesus made it abundantly clear that it would be better for one to "have a millstone tied around one's neck and thrown into the sea than to lead a child astray".

And finally, it is critical to note that some grave sins, such as abortion (which the churches consider *murder of the unborn*) should be **confessed** as Pope Francis has dictated - but should not necessarily be made *criminal*. To murder or imprison a 13 year old girl who aborted her unborn child might be a much greater crime. (And capital punishment is murder in many churches).

We have seen that Jesus declared only one sin to be *"unforgivable"* - cosmic arrogance/*hubris* to such a degree that one adamantly **denies that the spirit of God can forgive all and heal all**. We have noted how the *hubris* of Lucifer caused his fall from grace. The Bible tells us before humans existed, God created the angels - pure spirits/ pure energy. (In terms of nuclear physics, we might conceive of spirits and souls as clusters of pure energy - invisible and yet powerful - and capable of morphing into mass or "matter" when "slowed down" from the speed of light).

In many Bible translations, the story of an angel, called Lucifer, is cited: "How you have fallen from heaven, O, Lucifer, son of the morning". [Isaiah 14:12]

> "How you are fallen from heaven, O day star,
> son of dawn! How you are cut down to the ground,
> you who laid the nations low! You said in your

heart, 'I will ascend to heaven; above the stars of God I will set my throne on high; I will sit on the mount of assembly in the far north; I will ascend above the heights of the clouds, I will make myself like the Most High. But you are brought down to hell, to the depths of the pit".
[Isaiah 14:12-14]

It is thought by many theologians that when Almighty God revealed the creation of mankind, the fall of humankind, and His plan to redeem mankind by sending the Son of God (who would be born of His Holy Spirit from a human - the virgin, Mary), Lucifer rebelled! Lucifer felt too "superior" to humans to be forced to adore Jesus - a "mere human" even though the Son of God. We know that a (?*potentially* physical manifestation of God - the "Son of God") must have existed prior to the creation of humans because Jesus, Himself told the scribes and Pharisees: **"Before Abraham came to be, I AM".** [John 8:51-59]

Jesus commissioned 70 followers to preach and heal and when they returned jubilantly - saying: "Lord, even the demons are subject to us in your name", Jesus then revealed: "I saw Satan fall like lightning from heaven". [Luke 10:18]. Thus Lucifer (from the Latin for "the bearer of light") *became* Satan (from the Greek for "adversary") - the *enemy of God.*   Theologians believe Lucifer led a rebellion of angels who's **pride** would not allow them to adore the Son of God - as *human* -believing all humans beneath their status.

From the story of the first man and woman described on earth, we are told in Genesis how Satan tempted Eve and Eve tempted Adam to "eat of the tree of good and evil - and *then you will be like God*". They would have been so *proud* of themselves to be like God. [Genesis 3: 3-6].   Shortly afterwards, Genesis tells us the vegan offerings of Cain were less pleasing to God than the meat sacrifices of Abel. (More likely the plants were "not of the first fruits").   In our first recorded story of sibling rivalry Cain slew Abel and from this story we first learn of "sins that cry to heaven for vengeance" (*"peccato clamentia"*). "The Lord said to Cain ... the voice of your brother's blood is crying to me from the ground". [Genesis 4:10]

Besides murder the other sins that "cry out to heaven" include "the sins of Sodom". Although abortion is considered a form of murder of the unborn, Pope Francis declared it could be forgiven in confession.   The Catholic Church is not proposing life in prison or the gas-chamber in retribution - arguing that one sin does not absolve another. And although past theologians have interpreted the "sins of Sodom" to mean non-procreative sex, Pope Francis said in the documentary **"POPE FRANCIS - A MAN OF HIS WORD"**, "If a homosexual is seeking God, who am I to judge?".   And in the documentary **"FRANCESCO"** - Pope Francis says that homosexuals should be allowed civil unions: they deserve a family like everyone else. No one should be marginalized! A more progressive interpretation of the sins of Sodom comes from Sacred Scripture itself:

> "Behold, this was the guilt of your sister
> (city) Sodom: She and her daughters (nearby
> cities) had **pride**, a surfeit of food, and
> prosperous ease, *but did **not aid the poor and
> needy.*** They were haughty... [Ezekiel 16: 49-51]

Jesus, Himself, condemned the proud and haughty scribes and Pharisees who were so self-righteous:

"And as for you Capernaum: will you be
exalted in heaven? For if the mighty deeds
had been done in Sodom, it would have
remained until this day. But I tell you, it
*will be more tolerable for the land of Sodom
on the day of judgment than for you*".   [Matthew
11:20-24].

Jesus often condemned the pride and self-righteousness of the scribes and Pharisees more than any other sin. And he taught us to be humble. ***"Learn from Me for I am meek and humble of heart"***. [Matthew 11:29]

Chapter 4: Hopelessness

Is the glass half-full or half-empty?   It all depends upon your attitude.   In the 16th century, Saint Ignatius of Loyola taught his followers to meditate daily on *both* the positive as well as the negative aspects of each day in order to develop in them an attitude of *equanimity* (a balanced acceptance of the will of God) - together with an awareness of the necessity to *pray for strength* or "grace" to get through the negative aspects.

Sometimes the negative aspects or losses we suffer are so severe they lead to hopelessness and even suicidal thinking.   Hopelessness and suicidality are symptoms of a treatable **clinical depression** - *not* examples of "unforgivable sins".   Even the churches recognize this fact now.

Typically, psychologists and psychiatrists speak of *situational depression* and *major depressive disorders*.   If a person loses his/her job and the ability to pay the bills, it is common to develop a situational depression which would be expected to be resolved at the prospect of a new job which hopefully might even be better than the old job.

A major depressive disorder is not improved under such improved circumstances. Significant Cognitive-Behavioral therapy and oftentimes medications are required for its improvement. Sometimes, after a series of setbacks, it becomes impossible to "focus on the positive" without therapeutic intervention. And when hopelessness or suicidality is the predominant thought pattern, it is almost always necessary to employ neurotropic medications to restore neurotropic hormones which have been depleted by excessive stress.

Suicide is the death of an individual who intended to die when he/she self-inflicted an injury. It has been the 10th leading cause of death throughout the lifespan and has been the 2nd leading cause of death for those aged 10 to 34. Those struggling with their sexual identity have been extremely vulnerable - especially after suffering physical or emotional abuse from an ignorant community when they were the most susceptible to self-loathing It is significant that on October 22, 2020, CNN reported that Pope Francis declared support for civil unions for same-sex couples. This new attitude from the Catholic Church is a mind-blowing progressive attitude which can lead to the healing of such self-loathing suicidal underpinnings. In the documentary **"FRANCESCO"**, Pope Francis states: "Homosexual people have a right to be in a family. They are children of God and have a right to a family. Nobody should be thrown out or made miserable over it".

But suicidality is prevalent also among the bipolar depressed. These tortured souls often self-medicate with drugs or alcohol to alter their unbearable mental state. In the last decade we witnessed comic genius Robin Williams abandon his wife and children - hanging himself in despair after an alcoholic binge.

And some suffer prolonged unipolar depressions with agonizing torture from suicidal torments - seemingly unresponsive to multiple treatments. Recently **Esketamine** inhalation treatment has cleared such severe depressions in only a week. So it is critical to find the right psychiatric center for such life-threatening illnesses

Of course, everyone involved needs to help such souls - removing lethal weapons - providing social support - educating them on the new, miraculous therapies - and getting them enrolled into a therapeutic milieu.

Almost all Christian and Judaic faiths teach from the first 5 Books of the Bible, the story from the Book of Job. Job was a continuously good person who had prospered when the Devil was allegedly allowed to tempt him by destroying signs of his success after betting with God that Job would "blaspheme God to his face if he weren't surrounded by so many of God's blessings.

One surviving messenger after another arrived at Job's tent to inform him of a series of unfortunate events: e.g. "his animals had been carried off in a raid"; "lightning strikes had killed his sheep (and shepherds)"; "his herdsmen were slain and his camels stolen"; and "a hurricane destroyed many of his tents which were filled with many of his family - who died".

Yet after tearing his garment and cutting off his hair, Job cast himself upon the ground and uttered: "Naked I came forth from my mother's womb, and naked I shall go back again. The Lord gave and the Lord has taken away: *blessed be the name of the Lord.*" [1 JB 1:6-22]

There was no blaspheming of the Lord - even with the loss of all God had previously given him. It should come as no surprise that most of the intervening Book of Job is replete with grief - a natural consequence of significant loss. We would have expected a torrent of emotions like a tornado between rage against the elements (even against Almighty God - which we never got), and the anguish for the unfairness of it all - the bargaining to make the pain go away - possibly denial that "it didn't hurt that much" - and eventually an intrusive depression at the emotional bankruptcy and emptiness because he had invested so much loving energy into his loving family which he so cherished. We did get the abysmal depression of Job throughout that Book but Satan lost the bet. As if, at last, he had his "day in court", Job seemed to ask, after recounting his righteousness, "Why me, Lord?"

Fortunately for all who followed the story to the end, God made up for Job's goodness one-hundred-fold. Elizabeth Kubler-Ross has written of the normal stages of grief when one suffers such loss. She says one typically will amble through **denial, anger, bargaining,** and **depression**, before an **acceptance.** For instance, the death of a loved one challenges our coping mechanisms like nothing else we must face. We often regress and cope as we did in childhood - as if "forgetting" so much maturation we had acquired. Yet once we have "licked our wounds" as we must, it is possible to find mechanisms of survival *beyond* our last known capacity. We call this "moving forward" with our lives. Carrying the precious memories of them - of the happy times and images of their beaming faces - we are not "letting go" of our loved one but rather we are "moving forward" with all of this in our hearts

But what if we have been continuously complaining how "bad we feel" to everyone we see (as if it were the flu):

Moving forward means we examine our full range of feelings.   Are we **lonely**? - Even when we are around people ?   Is it a **comfort** to be around others?   Are we **worried** about how will all the chores get done?   Is there anyone in our lives who can assist us - without **imposing**?   Are we **beating ourselves emotionally**? - as if "we should have been a different person to our lost loved one? We can often work through these concerns in a Bereavement Support Group - often provided by the churches or a local mental health center.

Was this "another loss" among our "string of losses"? Are we **overwhelmed** by the losses throughout our life? A lifetime of losses may be helped by psychotherapy or medications. Should we discuss this with our doctor?

Can we openly discuss the emptiness this death has left in our hearts?   (Or is this just **another overwhelming emptiness**) that may require medications)? When we are continuously anxious with life's worries, we may empty the hormone "norepinephrine" in our brain. When we have poured out our "salve" hormone to soothe our worries, we may deplete this vital "peace hormone" ("serotonin") and we might have to replace these with medications.

We are entitled to be angry that God asks so much of us as human beings. But if **all** we show is our **irritability and rage**, we probably need professional help.

Looking back, can we see the gradual healing of our wounds after this devastating assault - losing a loved one? This is normal. If instead, we feel **hopelessly stuck** in our path of pain, we may need professional help - someone to talk to and help us see the positive steps we have made in our life. Before therapy, we may see the barnyard as an abysmal pile of horse manure. Psychotherapy helps us hope "there must be a pony to ride nearby with all that manure around us".

Can we accept the comfort and support and problem-solving help others want to share with us? Or are we **isolating** and **rejecting** the love others want to share with us? Do we say "*Yes, but ...*" to **all** their good suggestions?

Are we aware of the common physical complaints that come and go with normal grief? Or do we feel **overcome** by chronic pain that seems unbearable? This may require antidepressants.

*It is normal to lose some feeling of self-worth with the support of our loved one now **gone**!* Or are we **always feeling worthless** - this usually signals **clinical depression**.

Are we having our usual glass of wine or beer now? Watch out if we are seeking **daily alcohol** or opioids to "drown our pain". Can we work through occasional feelings of **hopelessness**? We have **clinical depression** and need professional help if we have **persistent despair or suicidal thoughts**.

Can we occasionally still experience some joyfulness in our lives – e.g., appreciating God's beautiful earth or the weather around us - or the joyfulness of our grandchildren? We are probably **clinically depressed** if we have **lost all enjoyment in things** which used to bring us joy.

In our journey through loss we see our minds attempting to cope with the violent disruption to our relationships and the loss of a loved one. Often our initial response is **denial** or disbelief. Another early attempt to cope might be **isolation** or actual withdrawal from the members of our community which are most needed at this time of loss . Like a wounded animal, we want to "lick our wounds". And these are stages of our "normal grief". Psychologists have discovered more mature defensive mechanisms for **coping** against this wound called grief - which may take some time to evolve, however.

Healthy **anticipation** is number one: don't anticipate danger: avoid fearful anticipation: expect joyfulness to come: accept peacefulness when it does arrive - even if only in small bits. "Choose peace over power". Think secure thoughts. Adopt a secure attitude: feelings should be expressed but without a bad temper - (even though anger is a normal reaction to loss). Be "self-led" not "symptom led". You *can* control your *inner* environment. You cannot control your outer environs. Put your mental health *first*.

Humor is number two. It has been described as "your best friend". Be sure to remember some of the "funny times" you had with your loved one - and don't be afraid to accept the relief of occasional laughter. *Excuse* rather than *accuse* others who let you down. Develop *objective thinking* rather than *subjective distortions*.

Suppression is number three: it is the brief, voluntary postponement of "falling apart": "work it down, not up". Feelings are facts and should be faced - but there is no crime in "holding it together" to help plan the funeral or guide the children in their loss, for example. (This is not the Freudian "repression" or virtual blindness to the significance of the loss).

Altruism is number four: consciously seeking the good for others - even at one's own risk (for example, those who choose the life of a firefighter). This is a Christlike response that usually doesn't come early after a devastating loss. Comfort is a **want** *not a need*. Choose long-term growth over short-term relief. Be *group-minded*.

Sublimation is number five: deliberately transforming personal pain into **kindness to others**. This is also something that comes late after a significant loss. Remember that every measure of self-discipline brings a measure a self-respect. **Have the courage to bear discomfort.**

We have learned that the emptiness of loneliness is eventually filled with our willingness to make strong **new** connections with other human beings and to rebuild the bonds of friendship with others as we communicate our many feelings with trusted individuals. But this takes time, of course. Eventually, we learn to even sublimate our pain into compassion and understanding for the suffering of others - which will raise us to a new level of maturity - a new self that brings newfound feelings of satisfaction. WE CALL THIS LEVEL OF GRIEF - **ACCEPTANCE.**

Depressed people make most of us "nervous" so our instinct is to "try to cheer them up". A person in mourning, however, needs time to resolve a loss and improves gradually when allowed to take the time required for this. During mourning, it may be difficult to "get out of bed", concentrate, answer questions quickly, and to care about daily living activities. Those mourners may be tense and irritable. Even in the presence of others, they may feel very "alone". It seems as if this condition of "shock" will last forever - but they won't be cheered up by someone who can't tolerate their sadness. This appropriate grief at the loss of a loved one does not have to be "stamped out".

Although difficult to endure, the sadness of grief can slow us down and allow us time to take inventory of what remains and assess what really matters as we move forward, regroup, and rebuild our capacities - and make realistic plans for the future.

On the other hand, clinical depression is a group of conditions manifested by long-lasting sadness or excessively deep depression which does not seem to resolve with time or improved living conditions. What differentiates clinical depression from normal grief is the presence of:

(1) **hopelessness** which persists;

(2) **suicidality** which may lead to planning;

(3) **worthlessness** feelings which are chronic;

(4) **guilt** feelings which are chronic;

(5) **"anhedonia"** - the inability to find enjoyment in the usual things which brought joy; and

(6) **intractability** - the inability to improve with usually supportive measures

The use of antidepressants during grief is somewhat controversial but they should never be withheld in fear the mourner will "miss out on the normal process of grief". Kubler-Ross has commented: "If only that were so!" Grief remains whether on or off antidepressants. Some depressions may require supportive measures, psychotherapy **and** medications. Intractable depressions have recently resolved in **just a few days** with medications such as **Esketamine** inhalation treatment. Many bipolar depressive states have improved on anticonvulsants such as **lamotrigine**.

We never consider clinical depression as "hopeless"!

Depression Scale: Short Form

Choose the best answer for how you have felt over the past week:

1. Are you basically satisfied with your life? YES / **NO**

2. Have you dropped many of your activities and interests? **YES** / NO

3. Do you feel that your life is empty? **YES** / NO

4. Do you often get bored? **YES** / NO

5. Are you in good spirits most of the time? YES / **NO**

6. Are you afraid that something bad is going to happen to you? **YES** / NO

7. Do you feel happy most of the time? YES / **NO**

8. Do you often feel helpless? **YES** / NO

9. Do you prefer to stay at home, rather than going out and doing new things? **YES** / NO

10. Do you feel you have more problems with memory than most? **YES** / NO

11. Do you think it is wonderful to be alive now? YES / **NO**

12. Do you feel pretty worthless the way you are now? **YES** / NO

13. Do you feel full of energy? YES / **NO**

14. Do you feel that your situation is hopeless? **YES** / NO

15. Do you think that most people are better off than you are? **YES** / NO

Answers in **bold** indicate depression. Score 1 point for each bolded answer.

A score > 5 points is suggestive of depression.

A score ≥ 10 points is almost always indicative of depression.

A score > 5 points should warrant a follow-up comprehensive assessment.

Source: http://www.stanford.edu/~yesavage/GDS.html

This scale is in the public domain.

The Serenity Prayer

God grant me the serenity
To accept the things I cannot change;
Courage to change the things I can;
And wisdom to know the difference.

Living one day at a time;
Enjoying one moment at a time;
Accepting hardships as the pathway to peace;
Taking, as He did, this sinful world
As it is, not as I would have it;
Trusting that He will make all things right
If I surrender to His Will;
So that I may be reasonably happy in this life
And supremely happy with Him
Forever and ever in the next.

Amen.

A prayer attributed to Reinhold Neibuhr (1892-1971)

Chapter 5: Reconciliation:

The greatest accomplishments of humankind have been achieved through ***communication*** and ***community***. One of the greatest tragedies of modern humankind is the **absence** of communication and community - our existential **loneliness**. Each of us needs to work at our ability to **connect with others and to communicate with each other.**

In spite of (or because of) social media excesses, loneliness has become our foremost mental health problem. Isolation during the pandemic and paranoid thinking that "any stranger can infect us" has only added to the problem.

Loneliness is the subjective experience of *anxiety* at the lack of *connection* or lack of *communication with others*. Some psychologists believe it is actually a painful, social *drive* to **seek connection** with others - as if we sense our social relationships have "become deficient". Of course, it is commonly felt with the physical loss of a loved one where it is called *grief*. But it can even be experienced in the company of others. It might differ from depression in that there may be more of a feeling of *emptiness* within us. Loneliness is common after moving into an unfamiliar community - when we usually call the feeling "homesickness". But loneliness can be present when we have relationships with others - even with family members - *if the feelings of love cannot be given or received.* This is the critical element in the solution for loneliness - **connection and communication in a dialogue for exchanging these feelings of love for one another.**

"You have made us for yourself, O Lord, and our hearts are restless until they rest in You". [Saint Augustine]

If we could learn from the lifelong struggles of Saint Augustine, we might discover that the greatest loneliness we can experience is the lack of connection and lack of communication - the absence of exchanging feelings of love - with our Father in heaven - Almighty God. Like everything else in life, "It's all about relationships". We are told as far back as Genesis: "It is not good for man to be alone".   Even Christ may have experienced this feeling momentarily when he uttered: "My God, My God, why have you abandoned me?" - quoting Psalm 22 while dying on the cross. It is noteworthy that Christ is not quoted as saying: "Ouch! These nails hurt!"

Loneliness is probably the most painful anguish one can experience - partly because it is so stigmatized - as if the lonely are "losers". Many of the elderly - especially during a pandemic, for example, are lonely through no fault of their own. Others are born with impairments in relating to anyone other than their mother (for example, some who are born with an Autism Spectrum Disorder). Still others are lonely because they have offended others - whether through attitudes of self-righteousness or behaviors such as insults or unfairness. If we are in that category, *it is within our power to make amends* - to ask for forgiveness and to reconcile our disagreements.

Since loneliness is the painful emotional response to separation, separation from our Father in heaven (our Creator) can produce our most intense anguish. Because man is a social being, it is usually necessary to reach out and establish a relationship with another *trustworthy being* with whom we can confide and share our emotions and experiences. An establishment of a relationship with God, a truly trustworthy being may be sufficient therapy for us as it was for the hermit monks over the past 2000 years.

If we have been overly narcissistic, we must never extrapolate that because "pathological narcissism is a fatal flaw in literary protagonists", it is therefore "unforgivable". Jesus made it clear that only **one** sin is unforgivable - having such cosmic arrogance that one denies the almighty power of the Spirit of God can **heal all and forgive all** the souls He has created.

If it seems daunting to reconcile with the "almighty Spirit of God, then establish a "best-friends-forever" relationship with Christ - who loves us so much he is willing to die for us (and did). It is likely Christ is the physical manifestation of God the Father who is pure spirit and so we would be establishing a reconciliation with Almighty God as well when we (1) confess we are sorry for offending God; (2) promise to do better; and (3) ask for forgiveness as we repent.

Jesus taught us the mechanism of all forgiveness - repentance or "turning from" our sinful ways. All who repent can and will be forgiven. All who can and do acknowledge God's power and willingness to be merciful - will be forgiven.

Besides the awesome parable of the **Prodigal Son,** Jesus told the story of the landowner who went out early to hire laborers for his vineyard. After all had agreed on the usual wages for a day's work, he sent them into his vineyard. But at 9 in the morning, when he saw others standing idle in the marketplace who were seeking work, he told them also to go into his vineyard and he would "pay them what is just".   So they went to work for him. Again, around noon and 3 PM he hired more with the same instruction. Finally, at 5 PM, there were still some standing in the marketplace and he asked them "Why are you standing idle all day?" They answered: "Because no one has hired us". So he sent them also to work in his vineyard under the same terms. And when it was evening, he told his foreman to gather his laborers so he could pay them - starting with the last hired and ending with the first he hired.

When the 5 o'clock hired workers were paid the usual daily wages, those hired first arrived and expected to receive more - but each received the usual day's pay. They grumbled against the landowner saying: "Those last hired only worked for one hour yet you have made them equal to us who bore the full day's burden and the heat". But the landowner replied: "My friend, I am not cheating you. Did you not agree with me for the usual daily wage? Take what is yours and go.   Am I not free to do as I wish with my money if I want to give the last hired the same as you? Are you envious because I am generous?" [Matthew 20: 1-16]

Isaiah explains: "For my thoughts are not your thoughts nor your ways my ways, says the Lord. As high as the heavens above the earth, so high are my ways above your ways and my thoughts above your thoughts." [Isaiah 55:6-9]   And Ezekiel argues: "You say, 'The Lord's way is not fair".   Hear now, house of Israel: Is it my way that is unfair or rather are not your ways unfair? When someone ... turns from the wickedness he has committed, he does what is right and just, he shall preserve his life; since he has turned away from all the sins that he has committed. **He shall surely live; he shall not die".** [Ezekiel 18: 25-28]

When the scribes and Pharisees surrounded Jesus to criticize Him for welcoming "tax collectors and sinners", Jesus told them the parable of the man who had a hundred sheep and asked them: "What man among you on losing one of them would not leave the 99 in the desert to go after the one lost sheep?   And when he finds it sets it on his shoulders and on arriving home calls his friends to tell them of his great joy.   I tell you, in just the same way: **"There will be more joy in heaven over one sinner who repents than over 99 who have no need of repentance".** [Luke 15: 1-10]

Our Bible continuously supports the mercy of God who forgives and rewards with paradise - even "death-bed conversions".

Moments before dying on the cross, while the "bad thief" was mocking Jesus for not showing He was the Son of God by "coming down from the cross that very moment" - the "good thief" humbly asked Jesus to "remember him when He entered into His kingdom".   Jesus promised the good thief: "This day, you will be with me in paradise". [Luke 23:43]

Chapter 6: Dream Big

Astrophysicist Ethan Siegel calculated that if the energy-mass at the moment of the "Big Bang" (some 13.65 billion years ago) contained just one *additional* proton weight, our universe would have collapsed upon itself "in its infancy". And, he continued, if it had contained just one *less* proton weight, it would have scattered into oblivion before even beginning to "grow its atoms" (let alone its stars and planets).[2223] You should therefore appreciate that our existence on this universe is no mere "*accident*". Albert Einstein is quoted as saying: "*Coincidence* is God's way of remaining **anonymous**".

We admit that life in the twenty-first century has become extremely stressful - whether because of anxiety over an early death through pandemic infection, loss of work through stringent public health measures, loss of funds for food, rent or mortgages, etc., or xenophobia that "the next person I talk to can give me COVID-19", etc.

Almost everything that happens follows the laws of physics - even what we call "*karma*" - what I do has a psychological effect on others and that will produce a psychological response from them. (This might be one way *hubris* brings its own downfall). The exceptions to the laws of physics are called **miracles**. We can pray for them because some events do break the laws of physics.

In this short tome (please see "**NORMAL MINDS**"; "**ABNORMAL MINDS**" and "**GOD SPEAKS**" or "**NORMAL SOULS**"), I have offered my thoughts on the science and philosophy of behavior. In "**NORMAL MINDS**" I presented eight qualities I deemed necessary for mental health. A mentally healthy person is *aware; positive; intimate; moral; responsible; self-controlled; self-confident;* and *integrated.* In "**ABNORMAL MINDS**" , we looked at the neurocognitive disorders that impair such behaviors.   In **"NORMAL SOULS" ("GOD SPEAKS")** we walked through the Bible viewing Genesis (see "In The Beginning" of this book); the importance of rest and play; the story of Job ("Keep Hope Forever"); the story of Moses and the 10 Commandments, the Great Commandment, God's promise to "shepherd His people"; the life of Christ (our "good Shepherd"); the many miracles of Christ (including the Resurrection as scientifically studied in the shroud of Turin) and the importance of "entering the kingdom of Heaven" here on earth.

The aim of this book is to emphasize the essential messages in "all of the above"; namely:

(1) Nobody is perfect - except God.

(2) Some of our sins "scream to heaven for
       vengeance".

(3) "Cosmic arrogance" is the only
       unforgivable sin if it means having a conviction
       that the Spirit of God cannot heal everyone
       and forgive all sins;

(4) Hopelessness is a symptom of a treatable,
       clinical depression (not an
       "unforgivable sin)

 (5) All of us get lonely at times and may have
       to work on our relationships.

(6) God's mercy will bring all who repent to eternal
       life in Paradise.

In some surveys, one-third of the population experiences loneliness. This painful emotion may peak at age 35 but is present at every age.   Holiday time may especially be the loneliest of all times with memories of who used to comfort and communicate with us but no longer can - and awareness that others could comfort and communicate with us but no longer do.

When, through no circumstances of your own doing, it becomes impossible for you to connect and relate to a trustworthy soul in your ambient surroundings or telephonic addresses - so that you can share emotions and experiences - then label this *solitude* an **opportunity to connect to God** - your Creator, Redeemer, and sanctifier.

Jesus has taught us that "eye has not seen, nor has ear heard, nor has it entered into the mind of man what God has prepared in paradise for those who love Him". So we are entitled to *imagine* just what **is ahead** for us in Paradise.

At death, we will be entering an energy field where souls/ spirits/ pure energy dwells. Some physicists have named a fifth energy field *"Quintessence"*. In 1998 two international teams of astrophysicists (one of which was headed by American astronomer Adam Riess) described what they termed "dark energy" (and which others have since labeled "transparent energy") - which constitutes 69.4 percent of our universe. (Only 4 to 5 percent of our universe is the stuff of which our bodies, planets and stars are made of). And 25 percent of the universe is dark or transparent matter according to the "standard cosmological model".

This energy field is called "dark" or "transparent" because it does not react with our ordinary triggers such as x-rays - but it exists by all methods of measurements and calculations. We know now that even the Higgs Boson (termed the "God Particle") exists and can be measured by pushing protons or ions to near the speed of light utilizing the CERN Large Hadron Collider (giving it a mass of 125 Gev) although it can seemingly "disappear" into "pure energy" at other times. And through the mathematical genius of theoretical physicist Albert Einstein, we have long known that energy and mass (physical "matter") are *interchangeable*. Energy becomes "mass" when it slows below the speed of light.

Then, can you imagine the "heavenly spirits or beings" traveling in the transparent zone at the speed of light? We call these angels and "saints" - those souls who have passed into the kingdom of God known as "Paradise". Astrophysicists have calculated there are 200 billion *galaxies* in our observable universe (as revealed by Hubble's Ultra Deep Field observations, for instance). And by observing the Cosmic Microwave Background radiation (the "ground-glass sparkling noise" on our original television sets when TV broadcasting ceased each night 70 years ago) - we believe an equal number of galaxies exist in our *non-observable* universe.

Now, assuming an average of 100 billion stars exist in each galaxy, that means that well over a billion trillion stars exist in our observable universe alone. And since our own Milky Way Galaxy is presumed to have between 800 billion and 3.2 trillion planets (though some galaxies are calculated to have as many as 8 trillion planets) - you should realize that as a "tourist saint" **you could spend an eternity just visiting and re-visiting "your favorite planets".**

So, eternity in Paradise should never get "boring". And we haven't yet even let you consider "getting to know God". Even if we have no eyes at first entrance into paradise, *we will know God* - somewhat as a blind person "knows" people and the surroundings about - only even better. Recall how you can know a personal friend through loving remembrances, current experiences, and persistent communication. In Chapter One we first described God as the all-encompassing *Array* of all that is energy/ spiritual; with continuous capacity to be physically present as His only begotten Son - a condensed yet separate "mini-Me" that can take the form of man - and an energy/spirit that can generate waves to communicate - whether through the glorified bodily senses (after the "end of time") or through such "resonance receptors" through which the angels and saints communicate. (Just recall that meson waves "tell us" just where the burial chambers of the pyramids are and "read stone" - like x-rays "read our body's bones"). As incomprehensible as the *"Array"* of God remains, it should come as no surprise that Jesus taught us: "If you have seen me, you have seen the Father".

2000 years ago, we "saw" Jesus. He was born in a stable, a humble person of humble birth; with a humble but holy human mother and step-father. He was an obedient child who became a working "carpenter" or builder before becoming a gifted teacher - who taught us everything we need to know to get to our destination - Paradise. Jesus condensed all commandments into his final message: "Love one another - as I have loved you". He taught us to love the lowly, the disabled, the poor, the demoralized, the outcasts or "disenfranchised" - *for theirs is the kingdom of Heaven.* Jesus was willing to die an excruciating death of crucifixion in atonement for our sins: we no longer need to sacrifice animals or "first fruits". And with his dying breath, he uttered: "Father, forgive them for they know not what they are doing" - thinking the best of us as we had just yelled at Pontius Pilate: "His blood be upon us and upon our children".

When we know God, we will know love and compassion - as we have never before known it. So even before our final judgment, we have "seen" Jesus - and therefore we have "seen" the Father. And we have also heard the warning Jesus gave us: "Strive to enter by the narrow door. For many, I tell you, will seek to enter and will not be able".

Just what is this "narrow door"? Jesus himself tells us that following His resurrection he will "come into His glory" and that all nations will assemble before Him, seated on His throne, surrounded by angels. He tells us He will then separate all of us into two groups: those on His right will hear Him say: "Come you who are blessed by my Father and inherit the kingdom prepared for you from the foundation of the world. For I was hungry and you gave me food, thirsty and you gave me drink, a stranger and you welcomed me, naked and you clothed me, ill and you cared for me, in prison and you visited me".

Jesus continues, the righteous will ask when did they do all these things for Him. He will answer: "Whenever you did these things for one of My least brothers or sisters, you did it for Me".

This may sound daunting on first reading. My personal belief is that no one can do "all that" except the late Saint Mother Theresa. So is it possible our merciful Lord will take into account that "feeding and giving drink to the hungry and thirsty" is nurturing our children or students (or parents when they are old) and giving money to our favorite charities or church; and that caring for the ill is taking care of our sick relatives/friends who are in need. And we can give our old clothes to the Salvation Army or to the Saint Vincent de Paul Society to "clothe the naked". We can vote for candidates who will make sure social services cares for those in need and who will provide programs that will be fair to immigrants. This is certainly something to *think about!*

REFERENCES:

[1] Lederman, Leon Nobel Laureate, BEYOND THE GOD PARTICLE, 2013

2 Tyson, Neil de Grasse, ASTROPHYSICS for PEOPLE IN A HURRY, 2017, W.W. Norton & Co

[3] Choi, Charles Q. OUR EXPANDING UNIVERSE, <u>SPACE.COM</u>, June 16, 2017

[4] Benvenuti, James; GOD SPEAKS; Lulu Press, 2012

[5] Rovelli, Carlo THE ORDER OF TIME, 2019 New York

[6] Darwin, Charles, THE DESCENT OF MAN; Great Books of the Western World, Vol49, Encyclopedia Brittanica, 1952, London.

[7] Genesis 1: 24-28.

[8] Barnett, Lincoln, THE UNIVERSE & DR. EINSTEIN, 1957, TIME, Inc.

[9] Genesis 2: 15-17

[10] Wisdom 2: 23-24

[11] Amos 5: 14-15

[12] Isaiah 49: 15-16

[13] Luke 15: 11-32

[14] Nouwen, Henri J.M., THE RETURN OF THE PRODIGAL SON, pp. 98-99;

Doubleday Image Books, New York, copyright 1992.

[15] Matthew 10: 41-43

[16] Micah 6: 6-8

[17] Matthew 5: 48

[18] Luke **15**: 7

[19] Ginott, Haim BETWEEN PARENT AND CHILD, 1965, Macmillan

[20] https://pro.psychcentral.com/exhausted-woman: July 8, 2017

[21] PARADISE LOST, Britannica Great Books 32, 1952

[23] THIS IS WHY OUR UNIVERSE DIDN'T COLLAPSE INTO A BLACK HOLE; Starts With A Bang; Ethan Siegel